For Susan Elliott

PUFFIN

Published by the Penguin Group
Penguin Books Ltd, 27 Wrights Lane, London W8 5TZ, England
Penguin Books USA Inc., 375 Hudson Street, New York, New York 10014, USA
Penguin Books Australia Ltd, Ringwood, Victoria, Australia
Penguin Books Canada Ltd, 10 Alcorn Avenue, Toronto, Ontario, Canada M4V 3B2
Penguin Books (NZ) Ltd, 182–190 Wairau Road, Auckland 10, New Zealand

Penguin Books Ltd, Registered Offices: Harmondsworth, Middlesex, England

First published 1997
1 3 5 7 9 10 8 6 4 2

Text copyright © Penguin Books Ltd, 1997
Illustrations copyright © Barry Smith, 1997

Filmset in Berkeley

Manufactured in China by Imago

A CIP catalogue record for this book is available from the British Library

ISBN 0–670–87194–X

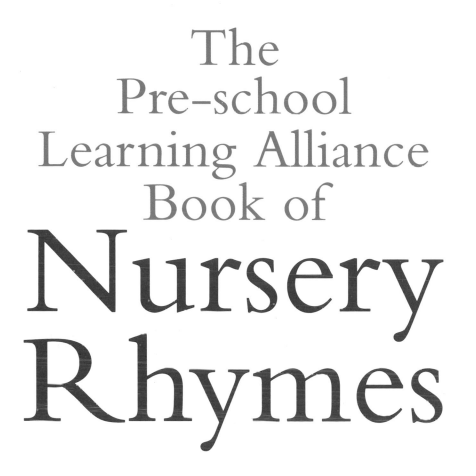

The
Pre-school
Learning Alliance
Book of
Nursery
Rhymes

Illustrated by
Barry Smith

Puffin Books

Hey diddle, diddle,

The cat and the fiddle,

The cow jumped over the moon;

The little dog laughed

To see such sport,

And the dish

ran away

with the spoon.

Incy wincy spider, climbing up the spout

Down came the rain, and washed the spider out.

Out came the sun and dried up all the rain,

Incy wincy spider climbed up the spout again.

Hickory,
dickory,
dock,

The mouse ran up the clock.

The clock struck one,

The mouse ran down,

Hickory,
dickory,
dock.

1,2 Buckle my shoe;

3,4 Knock at the door;

5,6 Pick up sticks;

7,8 Lay them straight;

9,10 A big fat hen;

11,12 Dig and delve;

13,14 Maids a-courting;

15,16 Maids in the kitchen;

17,18 Maids in waiting;

19,20 My plate's empty!

Eenie, meenie, Mackeracka,
Hi, di, dominacka,
Stickeracka, roomeracka,
Om,
Pom,
Push

Thumping, stumping, bumping, jumping,
Ripping, nipping, tripping, skipping,
All the way home.

Popping, clopping, stopping, hopping,
Stalking, chalking, talking, walking,
All the way home.

Three little ghostesses,
Sitting on postesses,
Eating buttered toastesses,
Greasing their fistesses,
Up to their wristesses.
Oh, what beastesses
To make such feastesses!

Five little peas in a pea-pod pressed,
One grew, two grew, and so did all the rest;
They grew . . . and they grew
. . . and did not stop,
Until one day the pod went . . .

POP!

Down by the station,
early in the morning,
See the little
puffer trains all in a row.
See the engine driver
pull the little handle,
Choo, choo,
off we go.

R
ain on the green grass,
And rain on the tree,
Rain on the house-top,
But not
on
me.

I
t's raining, it's pouring,
The old man is snoring;
He got into bed
And bumped his head
And couldn't get up
in the morning.

D
octor Foster
went to Gloucester
In a shower of rain.
He stepped in a puddle,
Right up to his middle,
And never went there again.

I hear thunder, I hear thunder;
Hark, don't you, hark, don't you?
Pitter-patter raindrops,
Pitter-patter raindrops,
I'm wet through,
I'm wet through.

I see blue skies, I see blue skies
Way up high, way up high;
Hurry up the sunshine,
Hurry up the sunshine,
We'll soon dry,
We'll soon dry!

Snowy, Flowy, Blowy,
Showery, Flowery, Bowery,
Hoppy, Croppy, Droppy
Breezy, Sneezy, Freezy.

A chubby little snowman
Had a carrot nose;
Along came a rabbit
And what do you suppose?
That hungry little bunny,
Looking for his lunch,
ATE the snowman's carrot nose . . .
Nibble, nibble, CRUNCH!

Little wind,
blow on the hilltop,
Little wind,
blow down the plain,
Little wind,
blow up the sunshine,
Little wind,
blow off the rain.

Blow, wind, blow!
And go, mill, go!
That the miller may grind his corn;
That the baker may take it,
And into bread make it,
And bring us a loaf in the morn.

Dancy-diddley-poppety-pin,
Have a new dress when summer comes in;
When summer goes out,
'Tis all worn out,
Dancy-diddley-poppety-pin.

Three little rats with black felt hats,

Three little ducks with cricket bats,

Three little dogs with curling tails,

Three little cats with bright red pails,

Went out to play with two little pigs

In satin vests and curly wigs.

But suddenly it chanced to rain,

And so they all went home again.

Where are you going,
My little cat?

I am going to town,
To get me a hat.

What! A hat for a cat!
A cat get a hat!

Who ever saw a cat with a hat?

To market, to market to buy a fat pig,

Home again, home again jiggety jig.

To market, to market to buy a plum bun,

Home again, home again market is done.

Hoddley, Poddley, puddle and fogs,

Cats are to marry the poodle dogs;

Cats in blue jackets and dogs in red hats,

What will become of the mice and the rats?

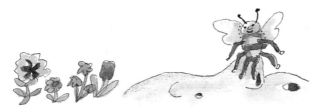

What do you suppose?

A bee sat on my nose.

Then what do you think?

He gave me a wink,

And said, "I beg your pardon,

I thought you were the garden."

Diddly, diddly, dumpty,

The cat ran up the plum tree,

Give her a plum and down she'll come,

Diddly, diddly, dumpty.

Six little mice sat down to spin;
Pussy passed by and she peeped in.
What are you doing, my little men?
Weaving coats for gentlemen.
Shall I come in and cut off your threads?
No, no, Mistress Pussy, you'd bite off our heads.
Oh, no, I'll not; I'll help you to spin.
That may be so, but you don't come in.

"One, two, three, four, five,

Once I caught a fish alive.

Six, seven, eight, nine, ten,

Then I put it back again."

"Why did you let it go?"

"Because it bit my finger so."

"Which finger did it bite?"

"This little finger on my right."

Little Tommy Tadpole began to weep and wail,

For little Tommy Tadpole had lost his little tail!

His mother did not know him as he sat upon a log,

For little Tommy Tadpole was now Mr Thomas frog!

Old Mother Hubbard, she went to the cupboard,
To fetch her poor dog a bone,
But when she got there, the cupboard was bare,
And so the poor dog had none.

Pussy cat, pussy cat, where have you been?
I've been up to London to look at the Queen.

Pussy cat, pussy cat, what did you there?
I frightened a little mouse under her chair.

Oh where, oh where has my little dog gone?
Oh where, oh where can he be?
With his ears cut short and his tail cut long,
Oh where, oh where is he?

Little Robin Redbreast

Perched up in a tree;
Up went Pussy Cat,
Down came he!
Down followed Pussy Cat,
Away the robin ran,
Said Little Robin Redbreast,
"Catch me if you can!"

A wise old owl sat in an oak,

The more he heard, the less he spoke;

The less he spoke, the more he heard.

Why aren't we all like that wise old bird?

Two little blackbirds singing in the sun,

One flew away and then there was one.
One little blackbird, very black and small,
He flew away and then there was the wall.
One little brick wall lonely in the rain,
Waiting for the blackbirds to come and sing again.

I saw a little bird

Come hop, hop, hop;
So I cried, "Little bird,
Will you stop, stop, stop?"
I opened the window
To say, "How do you do?"
but he shook his little tail
And away he flew.

One, two, three, four,

Mary at the cottage door;

Five, six, seven, eight,

Eating cherries off a plate.

Mix a pancake,

Stir a pancake,

Pop it in the pan:

Fry a pancake,

Toss a pancake,

Catch it if you can!

Pease pudding hot,

Pease pudding cold,

Pease pudding in the pot

Nine days old.

Some like it hot,

Some like it cold,

Some like it in the pot

Nine days old.

Who made the pie?

I did.

Who stole the pie?

He did.

Who found the pie?

She did.

Who ate the pie?

You did.

Who cried for pie?

We all did.

Georgie Porgie, pudding and pie,

Kissed the girls and made them cry;

When the boys came out to play,

Georgie Porgie ran away.

There was a crooked man,
And he walked a crooked mile,
He found a crooked sixpence
Against a crooked stile;
He bought a crooked cat,
Which caught a crooked mouse,
And they all lived together
In a little crooked house.

Rub-a-dub-dub,
Three men in a tub,
And how do you think they got there?
The butcher, the baker,
The candlestick-maker,
They all jumped out of a rotten potato,
'Twas enough to make a man stare!

Jack be nimble,
Jack be quick,
Jack jump over
The candlestick.

Sally go round the sun,
Sally go round the moon,
Sally go round the chimney-pots
On a Saturday afternoon.

Jack Hall,
He is so small,
A mouse could eat him,
Hat and all.

This is the way the ladies ride,
Clippetty, clippetty, clop.

This is the way the gentlemen ride,
Trippetty, trippetty, trot.

This is the way the farmers ride,
Bumpetty, bumpetty, bump.

This is the way the huntsmen ride,
A-gallop, a-gallop, a-gallop, a-gallop.

Tom, Tom the piper's son,
Stole a pig and away he run;
The pig was eat, and Tom was beat,
And Tom went howling down the street.

Ride a cock-horse to Banbury Cross,
To see a fine lady upon a white horse;
Rings on her fingers and bells on her toes,
And she shall have music wherever she goes.

There was a little girl, and she had a little curl
Right in the middle of her forehead;
When she was good she was very, very good,
But when she was bad she was horrid.

I can tie my shoelace,
I can comb my hair,
I can wash my hands and face
And dry myself with care.

I can brush my teeth, too
And button up my frocks;
I can say, "How do you do?"
And put on both my socks.

Teddy bear,
Teddy bear, touch your nose,
Teddy bear,
Teddy bear, touch your toes;
Teddy bear,
Teddy bear, touch the ground,
Teddy bear,
Teddy bear, turn around.

Teddy bear,
Teddy bear, climb the stairs,
Teddy bear,
Teddy bear, say your prayers,
Teddy bear,
Teddy bear, turn off the light,
Teddy bear,
Teddy bear, say goodnight!

Star light, star bright,
First star I see tonight,
I wish I may, I wish I might,
Have the wish I wish tonight.

Twinkle, twinkle, little star,
How I wonder what you are!
Up above the world so high,
Like a diamond in the sky.

I see the moon,

And the moon sees me;

God bless the moon,

And God bless me.